Heaven's Court System

Heaven's Court System

Bringing Justice for All

Bill Vincent

Heaven's Court System
Copyright © 2016 by Bill Vincent. All rights reserved.

No part of this publication may be reproduced, stored in a retrieval system or transmitted in any way by any means, electronic, mechanical, photocopy, recording or otherwise, without the prior permission of the author except as provided by USA copyright law.

Published By
Revival Waves of Glory Books & Publishing
PO Box 596
Litchfield, IL 62056
http://www.revivalwavesofgloryministries.com

Revival Waves of Glory Books & Publishing is committed to excellence in the publishing industry.

Published in the United States of America

Paperback: 978-1-60796-594-7

Table of Contents

Introduction 7
Chapter One Reclaiming Authority 11
Chapter Two Angels Released 17
Chapter Three Make Decrees 21
Chapter Four God's Judgment 29
Chapter Five Apostolic Breakthrough Decrees 37
About the Author 61
Recommended Books 63

Introduction

I'm telling you this is the most critical, pivotal time of all time. I really believe that there are things that are being set in motion, set in order hallelujah. Sometimes you keep going after something and the doors aren't opening, things aren't happening. You just keep going after it and you keep going after it and nothing seems to open up, what's going on? Does there need to be a decision made in the courts? I believe so. I began to search my heart for what God wanted to speak today and all of a sudden He began to speak.

God said the heavenly court, whenever that popped up God said court is now in session.

I don't care where you are in the things of God there are things about to open up like never before for the body of Christ. Decisions are about to be made specifically for your benefit hallelujah. Do you believe there's power in prophetic? There's power in prophetic decrees hallelujah. Part of the heavenly court is decreeing. The first point I want to talk about is prophetic degree.

I want to talk a little bit about this because if we don't know how to release decrees that really hit the mark we can declare anything we want, but if we don't declare decrees that are from God, we know they won't happen?

We need to declare what God want's to do for a season. It's God's mandate for this season, it's a revelation about heavenly courts. Sometimes we talk about the courts of praise. We really don't have a mind of understanding I believe as a church about what's really going on in heaven. I went into real detail in one of my books and some teaching in the past of the heavenly court system. I went line upon line and precept upon precept.

You don't want to preach all your old stuff all the time unless it's going to tap you in something new hallelujah. I want to talk briefly also about angels. We've had some angelic attention in revival meetings. We've had some angels coming, we've had some angels around and if you don't believe in angels you might as well forget the court system because guess what, who do you think causes the decisions made in heaven to take place? Angels are the ones who's working. Get ready hallelujah.

Also, we're going to understand the importance of making decrees to activate heavens court and the battle against God's plan and to bring restoration in our lives. God created Adam and Eve, but in the beginning to have dominion, remember they were created to have dominion in the earthly realm, to have authority to make decrees in the earth. You know what was happening whenever Adam began to be told to name the animals? He was speaking out words to cause them to be fulfilled. It was already, even Adam was given authority of God's mouthpiece. Everything that God did in the beginning He handed over to Adam to continue. He had the word of power.

Most of this is referring to scriptures to keep the prophetic writing going. We added a chapter for more of a scriptural reference at the end of this.

Chapter One
Reclaiming Authority

I believe we are supposed to still have that. Do you believe that? I really believe that we need to re-attain if you will, take back the authority that was given in the garden. I believe because of what Jesus did we have that right. Adam and Eve destroyed God's instructions. The devil succeeded in stealing their dominion. Known as a whole for the church the devil succeeded? There's a lot of beautiful people gathering together on Sunday mornings, a lot of people are gathering together singing a song, hearing a word, going home. The next week they do it again. People you know, people I know, people you love, people I love. The problem is, is they're living in a day of fallen Adam and Eve not a day of a resurrected Jesus Christ.

God told me this morning as I was... I had a lot of time, Tabitha was doing errands a few times and all of a sudden I heard God say this. Many within the church love Me, talking about Him, but many within the church don't know Me. It's become a charade. It's become nothing more than play actions. We have gotten as a church, as a whole have gotten away from the true gospel, the true power of God. I'm telling you God has gotten... Left out of the Church. Everybody's going around with that good old time religion, hallelujah. Give me that old time religion, old song we used to sing.

Give me that old time religion, hallelujah. I used to sing that song and thought I was going somewhere, hallelujah. You know what that song really should mean and I believe it might have when it was originally written before it was put in a hymnal, give me that old time religion back in the book of Acts. That's what religion was supposed to be. Turning the world upside down. Religion becomes dead instead of alive, hallelujah. I got to preach that, let's go on. I just feel Him right now.

To make matters worse disobedience of Adam and Eve caused all of humanity, all of us to suffer under one curse of sin to lose our dominion on the earth. Much hasn't changed, one man's decision can be a downfall for a whole lot of men and women. Sometimes you don't realize your decisions and how critical they are until it's too late. How many know Adam and Eve probably didn't realize what they were carrying upon their shoulders? Hallelujah but at the same time we could talk bad about it and we can even refer to that story as a fallen Adam and Eve, who had all they could ever ask for but yet wanted the one thing they couldn't have.

We can mock it, we can talk about it, we can refer to it, but you know what until you were put in that place, until you get to the place to where you are put into a place of paradise and told not to partake of one part, one fruit you cannot ever say I wouldn't touch it. There's things that I have been around ministers that they tell me I will never have an affair. A lot of times you know what, the reason is because they never had a chance. I never had ostrich, but nobody has offered it to me either, hallelujah.

We get to the place sometimes we think of ourselves higher and above everyone else but yet we have never been put in their place, put in their shoes. I believe what I'm doing right now is we need to redeem ourselves as a body of Christ for heavenly court to come back in session. We cannot have heavens court backing us if we are walking in the fallen. We all lost power to make kingly decrees but God did not leave us helpless. He sent Jesus Christ. I don't know how if we're alone this weekend, but we're just going to give it anyway. He sent Jesus Christ to rescue us. He gave us his living word to come boldly before the throne of grace to participate in a divine court system.

We are able to do that because of what Jesus did for us. God has given us a better dominion then in the beginning. Even what Adam and Eve did we have a better dominion then they had. Our dominion includes a spiritual dominion where we can take authority over the devil in the heavenly realm. We can take authority. You need to take authority over the devil in the heavenly realm. Sometimes you have to battle through. This is called heaven, do you believe that? Earth is heaven, do you believe that?

Doesn't seem like any heaven to me. It's considered Biblically a heaven. Where the devil is and all his cohorts are being in the second heaven. This is our temporary residence because they have a sentence where they're going to spend eternity in hell hallelujah. Except for the ones that's already been cast to the dry places. There's a third heaven where God is and all the angels and the supernatural throne zone. Hallelujah, a lot of times when you're pressing in and you're not really feeling the glorious presence of God it's because you're having to battle through that second heaven to get to the third heaven.

A lot of the body of Christ has given up and we have gotten complacent to where we're not battling through anymore. I'm telling you the violent need to take it by force. We've got to stop allowing the enemy to distract us and push us back. We have a God given right to call forth heaven to come down. We do. We have the right to participate in that court room. In heaven, where the devil accuses and God and his angels carry out justice. The devil accuses from his heaven and God releases justice from His heaven. Come on. Let me tell you something, when you line up to heaven's court, God's court, everything in heaven always overrides Satan's plans. It's a guaranteed court system if you go at it right.

Chapter Two
Angels Released

What I want to release about just for a moment is angels on assignment. You have angels on assignment. You have angels on assignment, an assignment specifically assigned to you and anyone who goes to the heaven's court. It's as though there are lined up angels awaiting aside the throne, waiting for decisions to be made. When those decisions get made God says go to Joseph. Let it be so. Angels freely execute the judgment of God echoed in heaven. Did you hear what I just said? Echoed, why is it echoed? Whatever you bind on earth shall be bound in heaven. Whatever you loose on earth shall be loosed in heaven.

When you declare the land that belongs to Revival Ways of Glory Shall come forth now in the name of Jesus as a decree that's gone forth that's been released into the heavens and because it's been released into the heavens it has caused an echo. What we have said here I feel the Holy Ghost, come on, it happens there. We're going to do it. Everybody says echo my words. In other words you decree, you release. My family shall be saved. I want to say it ... I'm getting ready to say it different.

It comes up into the heavenlies, Peter gets his catcher's mitt out, catches it says here God and God says let their family be saved. Echo. How many have ever heard binding and losing on earth as it is in heaven come forth like this? I'm telling you it's like God is saying there's more happening in that scripture then people have ever encountered. Some people don't know it, oh I'm sorry. I'm sorry. After a decision or a judgement is made in heaven a member of the divine council either serves as a divine messenger to announce the decision of the council or an angel will come to execute the divine judgment. It's as though when you release something from here to there and you know who you are in him you're a kings kid.

You have an authority to release that word into the heavens and because you have that authority angels have to work on your behalf. They're not working for you they're working for

Him. Prophetic decrees change from being your words because of that echo to his words. He still watches over his word to bring it to pass. King David writes prophetically, in Psalms chapter 103.

Psalm 103 verse 19 - 21, the Lord has established His throne in heaven and his kingdom rules over all. Bless the Lord, you His angels who excel in strength, who do His word heeding to the voice of his word. Bless the Lord all you his hosts, you ministers of his who do his pleasure. Angels work for God. When you release something into the heavens they go and do that which has been declared. That's their divine purpose. God said that there is an army of angels specifically designed specifically for his court system. Because the church hasn't really utilized them they are more eager then ever. Come on. Some of them have almost been on the unemployment line because they church hasn't been decreeing, calling things as though they are or as though they were.

We are to call forth those things that are not as though they are. Healed, set free, delivered, blessed, courts go. We've got to spend a little time on the court system, heavenly court system. If you go to a court here in America and they tell you you're fined $10,000 you know you're going to pay somehow or another $10,000 or spend some time in jail. When there's a decision made in heaven it's a done deal. Am I not changed immediately but it has to go through a certain procedure to get to you. If it's been ordered in heaven to repay what has been robbed and stolen and pondered from you then angels are set on assignment to redeem that which has been stolen from you and to get it back to you.

    I believe by the Spirit of God before we go any farther, those that will hear this, those are going to get paid back those things that have been robbed and stolen from you. The finances that was owed to you and due to you and things you should have you're going to get. The healing that you've been battling for it, haven't totally received get ready. Family that you have even had words saying they're going to be saved, it's time to call the heaven's court into business. I don't know about you but I want them to get saved not just saved for a day. It's hot in here. We need to talk about the heavenly court system.

Chapter Three
Make Decrees

Failing to accept our responsibility to make decrees that God has spoken hinders angels from entertaining or intervening the word of God in our lives. We've got to take responsibility and release decrees. God has opened our hearts up and said hey I want you to release prophetic decrees about those things which I've already spoken in your life. I want to release prophetic decrees about things you know that you're supposed to be having that line up with my word of God that's supposed to be a benefit to the word of God. Come on. If it lines up with the word of God then we can release decrees saying God's word as though it is. You need to prophecy to your life. We are called to make heavenly decrees and kingly judgments as ambassadors.

Did you hear that? Who's an ambassador? God's kids. I'm an ambassador. You want to hear something? I went to Florida one year, used to go all the time. Going to again when all of a sudden I'd go about the same time every year. Somebody gave me a time share to stay at a resort. That weekend before I left I preached ambassadors for Christ. I get there and they tell me there's a parking space I want you to use. I back into it, it says ambassador. We have a reservation. We have a reserved place in heaven as ambassadors why? Because you have a legal right. I don't think it was a mistake I believe God was prophetically speaking to me that day.

I back into that space, I look up and it says ambassador. I was like whoa, I'm supposed to be on vacation but I'm like back into the things of God, I'm like whoa hallelujah. How am I supposed to go to the hot tub now? Hallelujah? God wants us to stop making unrighteous judgments, to stop looking at situations through human eyes. You can look at your situation and it don't look pretty. Have ever looked at your finances and your bills and compared the two? It can really make you think. Thank God for faith. Thank God for miracles. Hallelujah. We've got to get to the place to stop letting unrighteous judgments come through our eyes.

We are making judgments against ourselves. That's what's happening and this is what God says he's going to make right through this sermon is as soon as you look at an area in your life and the enemy speaks to that and causes that mind to think that, that stinking thinking. Immediately you come into his hold. The decrees break that assignment. That's one reason why we are to bring every thought into the obedience of Christ. Until you make a righteous judgment and decrees about the situation God cannot release true breakthroughs that we desire. You say why? I've had breakthroughs before without decreeing. If God gave you a key and told you to use it and the door wouldn't open without the key His hands are tied.

God's saying there's your key. I'm giving it to you you've just got to open your mouth. Until you open your mouth and declare the word that He's already spoken, you stick it into it, you turn the lock, the door will open and it don't open until you use the key that he's given you. Amen. We're about to go up a level. Psalm 82:1 says this God stands in the congregation of the mighty. He judges among the gods, how long will you judge unjustly and show partiality to the wicked? You say what's going on? Why you sharing this? God is standing in the congregation of the earth judging among the mighty ones. You see that little G, gods? That's you, that's me.

We're the little G's. We are, why? Because we're of the heavenly court system. This doesn't take glory from him, if anything it gives glory to Him because you are an associate. If I ever say to you what up G? You know what I'm talking about. I used to have a guy I used to work with, he made chicken. He was our chicken fryer. Every day he walked by me he'd go what up G? I'd go what up P? I didn't know I just made up my own alphabet every day I had a different one. I was always G. I think he knew, he just didn't know that he knew. Hallelujah, praise God. The word here mighty is also judges, rulers or sons of God, mighty. God stands in the congregation of the judges, of the rulers, of the sons of God.

He's standing in the middle of leaders, apostles, prophets and the saints on the earth, ones like us who are entrusted with power to make prophetic proclamations, to make prophetic decrees. Because you are little G's you can say things and the big G's going to back you up. Echo, echo, echo. If you get a king and his son of a nation comes to the United States, and the son makes the decision the US has to back that decision. He makes the decision you have no rights to touch my car because I'm not of this country, I'm out of another authority.

They have to listen to the little G because of the association that he has with the king. Our nation has more understanding of God's governmental court then the church does. They get what is called diplomatic unity. All of a sudden next thing you know we can't touch them because they're of another court system. You are of another court system. You're not of this kingdom, you're of that kingdom. We're going somewhere, come on little G's we're going somewhere. He's judging our judgments and our proclamations to set the captives free.

He's judging our mercy to the widow. He asked how long will you judge unjustly. You thought I was going to skip that part, and show partiality to the wicked? The authority God has given us we as a church are judging unjustly. The church is judging one another instead of judging the crimes that has been done against humanity are things I wrote in that book the Rapture Revelations, talking about the abortions. Talk about an unjust. How many know the children don't have a choice? The day after sex pill, 16 year old girl should not be able to take a pill to give her ammo to have as much encounters with the opposite sex as she wants and she'll take a pill after and she won't get pregnant. It is nasty.

That's awful because the thing that happens is they don't protect themselves for sexually transmitted diseases. I could preach all night just on some of those things but I haven't got through where I need to be yet hallelujah. Life and death are in the power of the tongue to announce my word and the angels heed to the voice of your word in bringing about my divine judgment and justice. Because you are heaven's little G, all of us. The judgments we make happen in heaven and it becomes a divine judgment. God commands the mighty ones, I believe it's in verse three, defend the poor and the fatherless. Do justice to the afflicted and the needy. This opens up the realm of power evangelism.

You can go into the streets of a homeless, broken down man, minister the love of God to him and begin to decree into the court system on his behalf. You say why on his behalf? He is a man that has been broken and he doesn't have the keys to be able to make the decisions. He doesn't have an ambassador parking space. Come on. I believe we as a church need to rise up as a nation and do justice to the afflicted. Instead somebody homeless and smelly comes in and sits in a crowd and if the church allows them to stay they're usually alone in the corner. How many know there's an unjust thing that happened to them? What we are doing as a church is unjust.

We're to love one another. We're to help our brethren even the smelly ones, even the blue haired, even the Mohawk, even the ones with the short skirt. Come on. Now I have a standard that I'm trying to raise up for the ministry team itself but if somebody comes in in a halter top, guess what at least they're in the right place to get set free of something. I don't have to like it. I may have to look away but thank God I have a neck. At the same time, I would rather them come to church then do something out there. Guess what church, there's going to come a day in the days ahead, there's going to be more piercings, tattoos and clothing that is questionable popping in the church over the next years and it's because they're being drawn in by the Holy Spirit.

If we don't accept them when the Holy Spirit draws them then we will grieve the Holy Spirit. The Holy Spirit draws them and then we kick them to the curb. If they've walked in the door it probably took them a long time just to get to that place. If we reject them who knows how much longer before they walk through the door again. After I lived in a world of sin, when I walked into church I was walking in very slowly because I was terrified of God. I knew I had no business being in there but guess what, because of God's mercy and what Jesus did I had a God given right to be there. In verse six and seven God says you are judges and all of you are children of the most high.

Chapter Four
God's Judgment

You shall still die like men and fall like one of the princes. Judges refers to the supreme judges on earth and you and me. God is commanding us to bring forth justice on behalf of the poor and the fatherless. We are an abandoned generation of a fatherless generation. Nothing ticks me off more then a baby being born and the daddy taking off. There's a man in Tabitha's (my wife) side of the family, baby is born, beautiful girl. Wasn't born hardly at all and he walks out on the wife. You know why? The truth, trust me I checked with the spirit of God, he's jealous of how much attention the baby was getting over him. I'd have to repent but that's the kind of guys that I'd like to take behind the wood shed. Just give me ten minutes.

I believe in healing and resurrection so we'll be okay. God can I kill him so I can raise him up? The reason I'm saying this is because we are the fatherless generation. This is in the United States of America there are more children being raised up without fathers. It's hard. People don't know how hard it is. Let me tell you something, I'm going to say this and I say this with every fiber of my being, child support is not a replacement of a father. Even when you do give a little bit of money it's never enough to cover all that's needed for a child. How do you know? Because they want to play softball, they want to play volleyball, they want to play baseball, they want to play basketball, they want to be in band, they want to go to the moon. Next thing I think, can I have a sleep over on the moon? Hallelujah.

It does cost a lot and people don't realize that doesn't replace a man being a dad. I don't care if they give a thousand dollars a week it still isn't replacement. I believe it's in verse eight Asaph concludes his Psalm by pleading. Arise oh God, judge the earth and you shall inherit all nations. He invites God to bring his judgment back to earth because we are failing to bring forth justice. Did you hear that? God commands us through the prophetic decree to execute his divine judgment and justice. I'm telling you if you want justice to be done you're going to have to decree it. It would be better than having God come to judge America. You know why? Because we're associated with it.

Some of what's going on right now is judgment against America. The economy, it's ridiculous. In the books I name a few presidents and their wives because of the decisions they made. Listen, it's the decisions that I'm speaking about, it is. As soon as you sign on a dotted line to allow homosexuality to be a legal right there's things that our nation have been doing for a decade or more and just inviting the wrath of God back upon us. You say God's not that kind of way. Do you remember the days of Noah? Do you remember the days of Moses? If it wasn't for Moses, God would have annihilated the race twice.

Do you think ... think about what's going on in the church today. We might not have a molten calf in the middle of the sanctuary but we have built idols. The church has idols all over the place. I don't believe God will but I believe that a lot of the nation of the United States and the world deserve another flood. I don't believe it's Biblically, possible, thank God. Hallelujah, praise God. We are called to be mighty ones. God made us judges and it's God the king who rules who has made us judge. In other words he has handed you all authority. You have been given authority.

God has literally handed it over to you. He prepared a way in a place, a heavenly courtroom, a functioning court administration or system where He will and is to be executed. To participate in God's heavenly court system, to activate his saving, healing, delivering power on behalf of those who are bound and oppressed it takes a prophetic decree by us the mighty ones. Here we go, last wrap up. If a guy murders somebody in the United States he's innocent until proven guilty. In other words nothing happens until a judge, a little G raises that thing and hits it and says guilty. Doesn't matter how much evidence, doesn't matter anything.

It's until a judge makes a decision. You are the judges. The body of Christ are the little G's the judges. We can pass by a homeless person and we need to release decrees in the heavenlies. There's been injustices done to you and you need to make decrees to make justice where justice is due. Friends can make decrees of justice on behalf of others because there are injustices that have been done to you. There's been injustices done to you and we need to make decrees on each other's behalf and I'm telling you whenever we do we are making the judgment and God will echo the decision.

When any piece of paper in the United States is signed by a judge the only time that paper is not fulfilled to do that which it was signed for is when the big G (GOD) signs to counter it. The only time anything you decree will come back undeliverable is whenever God says otherwise. If you make a judgment that lines up with the word of God, God promises that we all be healed. God promised that we are supposed to be looking after the widows and the orphans and the fatherless and the homeless and the poor. We're to look on behalf of those that have been hurt and been wounded.

We are to look on behalf of the body of Christ. We are family, we are a group of body of Christ. We are joined together and we are supposed to be helping one another, lift one another and I'm telling you if it lines up with the word because of the position that you're in all of the court system will back you up. Come on. Received this? Hallelujah. It's time that we claim things as though they are. God is good. We give You praise God hallelujah. Give You praise, hey, okay. Every robbery that has been injustice we can call forth, judge it. Why? Because it's an injustice.

Every blockage the enemy's been able to do in your life is an injustice. All the witchcraft prayers that have come forth from the body of Christ, that's an injustice. Let me tell you something, you cannot use the ... you cannot use the court system of heaven in this sense. You cannot use the court system of heaven to bring pay back on those who have prayed witchcraft. What happens is it causes the injustice to bring justice in the injustice. That doesn't mean that something's going to get bad put on them. That's between them and God.

Praying witchcraft upon us or upon you or praying for people to be cursed or praying for people to be hurt, being sick, being afflicted, ministries to fail and all the prayers that have come forth from people that I know for a fact have come forth, that's between them and God. Let me tell you the number one thing I talked about in the very beginning of this, they will never have justice in any judgment until they repent. I'm telling you if you have prayed witchcraft prayers on anyone you need to repent. I want you to cleanse your heart.

I want you to start releasing decrees. It doesn't matter if I can hear it. Doesn't matter if your neighbor can hear it. Speak it out with your mouth through justice, sick and afflicted family healed, families saved. You might have seen somebody who's homeless decree justice. We have to understand the heavenly court God said is in session. If it's in session we need to take advantage of it. I'm not saying this because I'm the preacher I'm saying this because the Holy Spirit's the preacher. This is more than anyone can contain in an hour, hour and a half. There's some hidden keys in here we need to read again.

It's time to proclaim victory. Right now in the name of Jesus prepare our hearts that we cleanse our hearts oh God, that we make our hearts right before you so that we can cause judgments to be made. We don't want anything to be delayed because of things that are wrong in our hearts so right now in the name of Jesus as we repent, as we ask for forgiveness God, Lord just cleanse us oh God and then Lord we know that when we decree that all of heaven's going to back up the words that we speak.

We give you praise and glory that the heaven's court is now in session. We give you praise hallelujah, let's worship, repent, cleanse hearts, get ready hallelujah. Don't forget to decree some things hallelujah. I believe God's going to give immediate changes in some people's lives today, receive it.

Chapter Five
Apostolic Breakthrough Decrees
(Previously Published in Apostolic Breakthrough)

There are decrees and then there are apostolic decrees. There is a higher realm of authority coming through apostolic breakthrough. APOSTOLIC declarations, that are commissioned in heaven and sent by God, have tremendous authority to bring about His justice. The Lord will release significant breakthroughs when we declare decree and proclaim His will and His word. An apostolic declaration is a powerful weapon that shatters destructive plans of the enemy! It's even like a pre-emptive strike!

God began speaking to me about apostolic declarations. He highlighted this key scripture,
> *Isaiah 61:2 To proclaim the acceptable year of the LORD, and the day of vengeance of our God; to comfort all that mourn;*

He revealed mandates for the coming years and beyond is: to declare, decree and proclaim the acceptable year of the Lord, the year of the Lord's favor or Jubilee. He is anointing us to carry out this mandate! When we make a decree like Moses and the prophet Isaiah, it's like we're saying,

> *Deuteronomy 32:1 Give ear, O ye heavens, and I will speak; and hear, O earth, the words of my mouth.*
>
> *Isaiah 1:2 Hear, O heavens, and give ear, O earth: for the LORD hath spoken, I have nourished and brought up children, and they have rebelled against me.*

Did you know that Jubilee means total deliverance for us, cancellation of debts for each of us and our family and liberation from any kind of a bondage, taskmaster or oppression over our lives? In the anointing, we can proclaim "Jubilee!" and set into motion, like the laws of gravity, a power or a force of power that causes everything in our lives to begin to come into divine order.

Now, that's an anointing! We don't have to wait for the year of Jubilee! When God's word is declared, the angels of heaven act upon that decree and a supernatural endowment of power comes into our lives that we never had before. There's more! When the Spirit of the Lord God is upon us to proclaim "Favor!" Everything around us will begin to change because of the favor of God. One moment we don't have this power, and then in the next moment, under the anointing, we can proclaim, "Favor, favor, favor!" Suddenly, a download of favor comes that was lacking two minutes before, like a tangible 'coat of many colors,' dropping out of heaven as an anointing. We will see the results! Did you know that the same word for 'grace' is 'favor' and both words can be used in the same way? How many of us would just love a spirit of grace to come upon us today? God not only wants to give us favor, He wants to release the spirit of grace upon us, through a supernatural endowment of power.

It seems like everyone is trying to get favor, but there are principles involved that release favor upon our lives. First of all, God is a rewarder of those who diligently seek Him (Hebrews 11:6). God loves everyone the same, but the one who loves and seeks Him the most, is the one He will favor the most. God loves the wickedest, vilest sinner just as much as He loves us, but more of His favor is released to the one who deeply loves Him, who hungers and thirsts for Him. When we fail to seek God passionately, our favor level might not be the same as other believers who are pursing the Lord with all their heart. Jesus said to,

Matthew 7:7 Ask, and it shall be given you; seek, and ye shall find; knock, and it shall be opened unto you:

We can actually grow in favor by obedience and by diligently seeking Him. When we think about getting the favor of God, so often we think it's a process of getting into the favor. But levels of favor grow.

Jesus grew in favor with both God and men. When our favor with God grows, our favor with man grows.

> *Luke 2:52 And Jesus increased in wisdom and stature, and in favour with God and man.*

King David's life of devotion to the Lord attracted the heart and favor of God; Even though at times there were some areas of his life that were quite messy. It was like God looked at David and said, "But this guy has a heart of passion for Me!" When David became captain over about 400 discontented men, the favor of God became evident and this favor grew until the people made him King over Judah and all of Israel.

> *1 Samuel 22:2 And every one that was in distress, and every one that was in debt, and every one that was discontented, gathered themselves unto him; and he became a captain over them: and there were with him about four hundred men.*

> *1 Samuel 2:4 The bows of the mighty men are broken, and they that stumbled are girded with strength.*

So, growing in favor with God, hinges on our intense pursuit of Him. When God sees our love for Him and our determination to chase after Him with all our heart, He not only releases favor over our lives, He releases an anointing to proclaim "Favor!" You know, there's more than Jubilee and favor coming! Our day of vindication is coming, too! Now, let's go back in Isaiah to,

> *Isaiah 61:2 To proclaim the acceptable year of the LORD, and the day of vengeance of our God; to comfort all that mourn;*

The second part of that verse is to declare and decree the day of the vengeance of our God. He will release an anointing upon us so that we can actually call court into session and call heaven to be our witness, when there is injustice. It's an anointing to declare God's vindication (Definition vindication: defending against criticism or censure [Webster's Dictionary]).

We can access the heavenly court system where the Holy Ghost presides as our advocate and counselor in matters concerning our lives, destiny, inheritance and death. How many of us would like God to take up our cause right now? There are circumstances in our lives sickness, disease, death, poverty, bondage, oppression, false accusations that we know are not God's will for us. Yes, we can think of all kinds of injustice, but the Spirit of the Lord is upon us to declare vindication. We know the scripture where God says "Vengeance is Mine, I will repay," says the Lord, but He has invited us, as saints of God, into a place of power of the decree.

> *Hebrews 10:30 For we know him that hath said, Vengeance belongeth unto me, I will recompense, saith the Lord. And again, The Lord shall judge his people.*

We can actually approach the heavenly court system; not only to gain justice on our behalf, but also to petition God for divine judgment against our enemies. God will plead the cause of His people, but we have to learn how to ascend the courts of heaven. As children of God we have a right to see injustice removed and it will be removed when we declare and proclaim God's word, His truth. God's word prevails and disarms injustice!

Now, let's examine some background scriptures so we can more fully understand how our decrees disarm injustice in the heavenly realm. The heavenly court system is known by other names in scripture:
a) Divine council?
Psalms 82:1
b) Counsel of El (God)?
Job 15:8
c) The council of Yahweh?
Jeremiah 23:18
d) Council of the holy ones?
Psalms 89:7

I'd like to define divine 'council,' and divine counsel. When a group meets together like an administrative, advisory or legislative body for discussion and advice, we call this grouping, a council. So, when the heavenly court is in session, the members of the court form a body called the divine council. But, when these members of the divine council listen to the Lord's message and engage in discussion, the members are hearing God's advice and

wisdom and His divine counsel. Below, I will list some of the members of the divine council:
a) God
b) The Hosts of heaven also called the stars of heaven: "They fought from the heavens; The stars from their courses fought against Sisera" Judges 5:20 (The hosts of heaven include: the angels: the Cherubim and the Seraphim, Michael, the archangel, who is the leader of angels in battle and the archangel over the nation of Israel and Gabrielle, who brings interpretation of divine revelation concerning times and season of the church.)
c) The cloud of witnesses: the apostles, prophets and saints of old
d) The prophets that are alive on the earth and believers
e) The twelve disciples who judge the nation of Israel
f) The 24 elders
g) Devils

The divine counsel of God is described differently in several places in scripture. The heavenly courts can be found on earth or in heaven and both the counsel and council of God are always linked to the dwelling place of God. It can happen in the mountain it can happen in the temple setting:
a) The mound of the congregation:
Isaiah 14:13
b) The holy mountain of God:
Ezekiel 28:14
c) An earthly picture linked to the
tent or Tabernacle of God:
Isaiah 33:20

When he comes before the throne in the spirit, the apostle John sees God, sitting on the throne, like jasper stone and sardius in appearance. He sees a beautiful scene of worship.

> *Revelations 4:1-11 After this I looked, and, behold, a door was opened in heaven: and the first voice which I heard was as it were of a trumpet talking with me; which said, Come up hither, and I will shew thee things which must be hereafter. And immediately I was in the spirit: and, behold, a throne was set in heaven, and one sat on the throne. And he that sat was to look upon like a jasper and a sardine stone: and there was a rainbow round about the throne, in sight like unto an emerald. And round about the throne were four and twenty seats: and upon the seats I saw four and twenty elders sitting, clothed in white raiment; and they had on their heads crowns of gold. And out of the throne proceeded lightnings and thunderings and voices: and there were seven lamps of fire burning before the throne, which are the seven Spirits of God. And before the throne there was a sea of glass like unto crystal: and in the midst of the throne, and round about the throne, were four beasts full of eyes before and behind. And the first beast was like a lion, and the second beast like a calf, and the third beast had a face as a man, and the fourth beast was like a flying eagle. And the four beasts had each of them six wings about him; and they were full of eyes within: and they rest not day and night, saying, Holy, holy,*

holy, Lord God Almighty, which was, and is, and is to come. And when those beasts give glory and honour and thanks to him that sat on the throne, who liveth for ever and ever, The four and twenty elders fall down before him that sat on the throne, and worship him that liveth for ever and ever, and cast their crowns before the throne, saying, Thou art worthy, O Lord, to receive glory and honour and power: for thou hast created all things, and for thy pleasure they are and were created.

Later, in the book of Revelation chapters five through eight, although the setting remains the same the very throne of God, the scene changes to a courtroom that releases judgment.

As Christians, we often have a mental picture of two distinct places in heaven: one, the throne room where the saints worship and two, the courtroom of God where judgments are made. However, in the book of Revelation, it appears that both worship and judgment happen in the same place, just at different times. In the throne room John sees and refers to each member of the Trinity. Firstly, he identifies God as "One sitting on the throne." (Revelation 5) as the Lion of the Tribe of Judah, the great overcomer. There it is the Trinity: Father, Son and Holy Ghost, in the throne room! The prophet, Daniel, gives one of the best descriptions of the throne room to be found in scripture; both the Ancient of Days and the Son of Man are seen together in their governmental authority:

> *Daniel 7:9, 10 I beheld till the thrones were cast down, and the Ancient of days did sit, whose garment was white as snow, and the hair of his head like the pure wool: his throne was like the fiery flame, and his wheels as burning fire. A fiery stream issued and came forth from before him: thousand thousands ministered unto him, and ten thousand times ten thousand stood before him: the judgment was set, and the books were opened.*

In the above passage, Daniel identifies the Ancient of Days as the one presiding over judgment and the Son of Man, Jesus Christ, receiving His glorious kingdom. Both Daniel and John describe the presence of the Lamb of God. Revelation 4 and Ezekiel 1 and 10 describe the throne, but in two different ways.

The Apostle John refers to a throne on the ground, on the sea of glass like crystal. On the other hand, in his vision, Ezekiel looks up to the throne through the firmament. He sees the throne, moving on wheels within the wheels and covered in eyes. Again, both prophetic books speak of four living creatures, but in different ways. Although Revelation doesn't speak of a throne with wheels, Ezekiel describes four living creatures that actually create a celestial chariot for the throne to ride on.

That's why the throne has wheels, it moves. Did you know the throne of God rides on a chariot with wheels and that the four living creatures actually form part of the chariot that carries the throne? It's a prophetic picture of the

Levitical priests who carried the Ark of the Covenant, which was a symbol and actual sign of God's presence. Where the ark went, so did the presence of God.

1 Chronicles 15:2 Then David said, None ought to carry the ark of God but the Levites: for them hath the LORD chosen to carry the ark of God, and to minister unto him for ever. Whenever we talk about the throne room we should picture it like the tabernacle of Moses (Exodus Chapter 35 to 38) and the temple of Solomon (1 Kings Chapter 6 to 8) all the tabernacle imagery. We can think of every reference to the throne of God as a reference to the ark of God as well both symbolize the presence of God, the place where God was. Also, both the ark and the throne moved as God's presence moved.

The divine council room, also called the heavenly court, is situated in the Throne Room. Remember, it's a place where judgments are decided upon, but it also functions as a throne room of worship. Let's keep in mind that the devil can come before the throne of judgment, bringing accusations against believers, but he doesn't have access to the throne room of worship. One descriptive scene of demonic involvement in the council room is found in,

> *1 Kings 22:19-23 And he said, Hear thou therefore the word of the LORD: I saw the LORD sitting on his throne, and all the host of heaven standing by him on his right hand and on his left. And the LORD said, Who shall persuade Ahab, that he may go up and fall at Ramothgilead? And one said on this manner, and another said on that manner. And*

there came forth a spirit, and stood before the LORD, and said, I will persuade him. And the LORD said unto him, Wherewith? And he said, I will go forth, and I will be a lying spirit in the mouth of all his prophets. And he said, Thou shalt persuade him, and prevail also: go forth, and do so. Now therefore, behold, the LORD hath put a lying spirit in the mouth of all these thy prophets, and the LORD hath spoken evil concerning thee. This portion of scripture gives us a picture of a court session going on in heaven. Micah, the prophet, begins by describing the Lord sitting on His throne, surrounded by the host of heaven. We read that an evil spirit answers the Lord's question. "Who will persuade Ahab to go up, that he may fall at Ramoth Gilead?" The demon comes forward, replying: "I will persuade him. I will go out and be a lying spirit in the mouth of his prophets." Then the Lord gives permission to the evil spirit: "You shall persuade him and also prevail. Go out and do it." So, even evil spirits, at times, can be a part of the divine council of heaven to accomplish God's will! But evil spirits don't have the last say! We have a part in judgment against our adversary the devil, who is constantly battling against prosperity coming into our lives.

Although we need God to bring judgment, He invites us to be involved in the divine counsel concerning our life and death, our fate and inheritance. The past biblical and spiritual leaders, had access to the divine council room.

Joshua, one such leader, was seen by Zechariah standing before the Lord in the heavenly courts. After satan's unsuccessful attempt to oppose Joshua and after his filthy garments were replaced by rich robes, here's what the Lord said to him.

> *Zechariah 3:7 Thus saith the LORD of hosts; If thou wilt walk in my ways, and if thou wilt keep my charge, then thou shalt also judge my house, and shalt also keep my courts, and I will give thee places to walk among these that stand by. Joshua was given access to walk among heavens council. Also, we can see, after examining the life of the prophet, Jeremiah, that he was a godly, righteous, man of God who stood in the counsel of the Lord and then pronounced God's judgments.*

In the following verses, even though God is asking the question: "For who has stood in the counsel of the Lord and has perceived and heard His word?" We can safely identify Jeremiah as one who stood in the counsel of the Lord while God's judgments were pronounced on the wicked:

> *Jeremiah 23:18-20 For who hath stood in the counsel of the LORD, and hath perceived and heard his word? who hath marked his word, and heard it? Behold, a whirlwind of the LORD is gone forth in fury, even a grievous whirlwind: it shall fall grievously upon the head of the wicked. The anger of the LORD shall not return, until he have executed, and till he have performed the thoughts of*

> *his heart: in the latter days ye shall consider it perfectly.*

Angels freely execute the judgments of God echoed in heaven after we decree what God has spoken to us on the earth.

After a decision or judgment is made in heaven, a member of the divine council either serves as a divine messenger to announce the decision of the council or an angel will come to execute the divine judgment. King David writes prophetically about the ministry of angels:

> *Psalms 103:19-21 The LORD hath prepared his throne in the heavens; and his kingdom ruleth over all. Bless the LORD, ye his angels, that excel in strength, that do his commandments, hearkening unto the voice of his word. Bless ye the LORD, all ye his hosts; ye ministers of his, that do his pleasure.*

Failing to accept our responsibility to make the decrees that God has spoken hinders angels from intervening in our lives. We are called to make heavenly decrees or kingly judgments as His ambassadors. However, God wants us to stop making unrighteous judgments, to stop looking at situations through human eyes.

Until we make righteous judgments and decrees about situations, God cannot release the true breakthroughs we desire! Here's what the Lord said about His people's judgments:

Psalms 82:1 A Psalm of Asaph. God standeth in the congregation of the mighty; he judgeth among the gods.

God is standing in the congregations of the earth, judging among the mighty ones or little "g"----gods, you and me. The word here for mighty is also judges, rulers or sons of God. So, He's standing in the middle of the leaders, apostles, prophets and saints on the earth, ones like us, who are entrusted with power to make prophetic decrees and proclamation. He's judging our judgments, our proclamations, to set the captives free; He's judging our mercy to the widow and to the poor. He asks, "How long will you judge unjustly and show partiality to the wicked?" It's like He's saying, "Haven't I made you my judges? Have I not made you sons of God in the earth?

I've given you power through the prophetic decree. Life and death are in the power of the tongue to announce My word and the angels heed to the voice of your word in bringing about My divine judgment and justice." God commands the mighty ones in verse three: "Defend the poor and the fatherless. Do justice to the afflicted and needy." And then in verse six, God says, "You are judges and all of you are children of the Most High, you shall still die like men and fall like one of his princes." Judges refers to the supreme judges here on the earth as you and me. Clearly, God is commanding us to bring forth justice on behalf of the poor and the fatherless. We are called, with great responsibility and power, to make judgments through the prophetic decree against the enemy.

Asaph concludes his Psalm by pleading with God:
Psalms 82:8 Arise, O God, judge the earth: for thou shalt inherit all nations. He invites God to bring His judgment back into the earth because we are failing to bring forth justice.

But God command us, through the prophetic decree, to execute His divine judgment and justice. Although we are called the mighty ones, and God made us judges, it's God, the King, who rules! He prepared a way and a place, a heavenly courtroom and a functioning heavenly court administration or system, where His will is to be executed. But, to participate in God's heavenly court system, to activate His saving, healing, delivering power on behalf of those who are bound and oppressed, it takes a prophetic decree by us, the mighty ones.

Several scriptures in the book of Job reveal the power of the prophetic decree, expressed through Job's friend, Eliphaz:

Job 22:27-29 *Thou shalt make thy prayer unto him, and he shall hear thee, and thou shalt pay thy vows. Thou shalt also decree a thing, and it shall be established unto thee: and the light shall shine upon thy ways. When men are cast down, then thou shalt say, There is lifting up; and he shall save the humble person.*

Job's friend understood the heart of God when he said, "You will decree a thing and it will be established" and "When they cast you down and you declare." This scripture gives us the key to victory declaring God's will! Our breakthroughs are released when we obediently declare God's will; our words activate angels to heed the voice of His word. So, when we declare God's will that prosperity and healing or exaltation will come and victory or favor will come we actually release God to save the humble. Remember, God shall plead the cause of His people.

As stewards and members of the heavenly court or divine council, when we declare and sing in faith, "Exaltation will come," then He will come and save the humble person. He will deliver the one, even the one who is not innocent, at our decree.

Believers who place great value on what God values bring great delight to Him. Listen! He gave us the opportunity to be channels that release His saving, healing and delivering power, when we declare His word and His will. This is no small thing in His sight! But, today if we fail to proclaim liberty to the captives and recovery of sight to the blind, then their destiny is jeopardized, robbed and plundered. Isaiah expresses God's heart when he writes:

Isaiah 42:22 But this is a people robbed and spoiled; they are all of them snared in holes, and they are hid in prison houses: they are for a prey, and none delivereth; for a spoil, and none saith, Restore.

You know what? Now days, we're not doing a very good job speaking healing words to the sick, proclaiming liberty to the captives or decreeing freedom for the prisoners. (Our destiny is adversely affected, too, when we neglect to decree God's word and His will.) That's why God was judging the mighty ones in Psalms 82; He was saying, "You're not taking care of the poor, the needy and the afflicted. You're not making decrees of justice." There are believers in the church today, caught in addiction and bondage, hidden in prison houses. There's so much defeat! If we're honest, we'll admit that there are times when our back is up against the wall. We think, "Hey, I know who's going to win in the end, but I'm losing right now and I don't know what's going on!" Yet, when we start to rise up in authority, making declarations to set captives free, we're still not seeing the victory we're contending for. Our problem is not in the words we decree, but in the faith behind them. We often don't really believe that there really is authority and power in our words.

God is actually hindered from saving the humble and wreaking vengeance on the enemy when we don't understand the power in the declarations: "Exaltation will come," and "Decree a thing and it will be established" (Job 22:28, 29). We must learn how to approach the heavenly courtroom and utilize the provision God made for us there in that setting. Remember, the angels either announce or execute the decisions made in the heavenly court. These heavenly ministries carry out our earthly prophetic decrees which line up with the truth of God's word and His will. So, God wants to save and bring restoration to the humble! I believe that His power to restore is set into motion when we declare: "Restore!" "Restore!" Then the angels in heaven are released to execute this righteous and just decree!

We're in a battle right now! We're being prevailed against! So often our back is up against the wall and we're getting the short end of the stick. Some of us are losing in the fight against sin and sickness, disease and death. We're contending for prosperity and fulfillment of the prophetic word in our lives. The fight is on for our kids to know Jesus. We're fighting for that mortgage that land, that property. This war has raged for centuries! The prophet, Daniel saw this war we would face today: "I was watching; and the same horn was making war against the saints and prevailing against them" (Daniel 7:21). This was is with the antichrist or the anit-anointing spirit. It reminds us of the battle outlined in Daniel 10 about the Prince of Persia opposing Michael the archangel for 21 days. As the enemy opposed Daniel, the anti anointing and anti-christ spirits oppose our every destiny and inheritance in God UNTIL....

> *Daniel 7:22 Until the Ancient of days came, and judgment was given to the saints of the most High; and the time came that the saints possessed the kingdom.*

When the Ancient of Days comes to execute judgment on our behalf, we will have justice in our lives. Today could be the day! Right now, we could ascend the courts of heaven, approach the Ancient of Days, Judge and present our case! We could begin to act as sons of God on the earth with the power of apostolic declaration in our mouth! As we say "Exaltation will come!" We release God to save the humble and to deliver those who are bound. When we say, "Restore!" we release God's 'repairer of the breach' anointing (Isaiah 58:12) which will cause everything in our lives that is lost and broken to be restored not just double, not just five times, but seven times the thief must repay God's people. Restoration will happen when we declare, "Restore!" "Restore!" "Exaltation will come!"

Before we begin to approach the heavenly courts, I want you to think about every case that you have right now, and every area of your life that you are waiting for a breakthrough. It could be that the Devil is keeping you from receiving your inheritance and stepping into your destiny. Or your difficulty might be concerning your health; he is bringing sickness and disease by stealing, killing and destroying. Any areas of your life right now where you know there is injustice and you've tried to battle it through yourself think about your case. Maybe you're trying to defend yourself by bringing vengeance by yourself. You need God to plead your cause. When we petition the Ancient of Days in just a moment with our case, the angels are going to heed to the voice of His word spoken by us, the saints. Remember, whenever a decision is made, a member of the divine counsel either serves as a messenger to announce the decision of the counsel, or an angel will come to execute the divine judgment, so that the justice of God can come.

The Old Testament Church was entrusted by God to bring about judgments in their own courts in five matters: life, death, destiny, kingship or inheritance. (You know they had their own courts. Remember when they took Jesus before Pontius Pilate? There were certain boundaries to the courts that the Pharisees, Sadducess and Jews had and so they turned Jesus over to the Romans or how they wanted to stone the woman who was caught in adultery.) Now if you can think of any area of your life right now that you are not living in the fullness of the promise and word of God in these five areas, you have a right today to ascend the courts of heaven and petition the Ancient of Days to come and pronounce judgment in your favor. I've been in meetings when the Lord gave us permission to make decrees resulting in numerous testimonies coming out after. Supernaturally several people had thousands of dollars appear in their bank account right after the service!

God is inviting you to approach His throne to present your case right now. We can petition God together for His judgment and make apostolic declarations and decrees. Remind God of the prophetic promises you received and then name each injustice. Now listen, God is also entrusting us today to begin proclaiming liberty to the captives and the opening of the prison to those who are bound. We can say "Restore!" and "Exaltation will come!" We can begin to bring justice and mercy for the poor and needy, the afflicted and the widow, with the word of God in our mouths. He gave us authority to set the captives free, in Jesus' Mighty name! Now pray with me to execute judgment on earth and to proclaim God's favor in our lives:

God, today, we are petitioning the court of heaven and we are petitioning you, the one who is faithful and just, the one who is true!

The Holy ones today are approaching the courtroom in heaven where judgment is made; divine judgment for divine justice on behalf of the bound and the afflicted and the oppressed. Thank you, Lord, that today we can stand in the council of heaven as prophetic voices, as mighty ones and judges and rulers on this earth with dominion to make the decree. Today, Ancient of Days, with all respect we come before your throne and we make petitions and we make requests. God, together we are petitioning the council members in heaven right now, requesting that the host of heaven begin to hear, with You, the Ancient of Days upon Your throne, concerning where we need Your divine judgment and Your vindication to come. You are the God who rolls back the reproach. You are the God who pleads the cause of your people, the God who pronounces judgment and favor over the saints of the Most High. We petition You today in intercession and we present our cases. Hear them, Please God!

Let the courts of heaven be open right now and let the session come into place right now. We pray that you would come into our homes and congregations into the midst of the might ones. God we are going to make a decree: Exaltation will come! Restore! Restore! Restore! God we loose it in heaven. Restore! Restore! Restore! Divine order coming now. In every area where there has been stealing and killing and destroying we speak the word of the Lord. We say over that loss, Restore! Devil, give it all back! The thief and the liar give it all back! God, we believe You will restore and we claim it! God, we ask for it! We declare it! God, we proclaim the day of your vengeance. We proclaim that this is the year of Your favor! This is the year of the Lord's favor! This is the year! This is our acceptable year, liberation and Jubilee! Lord, I say it over the people today: Favor! Favor! Favor! Divine Favor! I proclaim and I decree: Favor! Favor! Favor! The vengeance of God! The vengeance of God! How I can feel the Glory!

Now, Lord let the angelic hosts who execute your judgment go forth. Let the warring angels act to defeat the enemy and restore our kingly destiny. Let them overcome in the spirit-world, in Jesus name! And let the angelic hosts overcome every demonic power or stronghold and every assignment that is aimed against our inheritances! We throw it down! We take authority concerning our kingship over every power that resists. We know O god, that You must come and make a judgment in favor of the saints; that's what we need right now. We thank you, Lord, today for the victory!

About the Author

Bill Vincent is no stranger to understanding the power of God. Not only has he spent over twenty years as a Minister with a strong prophetic anointing, he is now also an Apostle and Author with Revival Waves of Glory Ministries in Litchfield, IL. Along with his wife, Tabitha, he, leads a team providing apostolic oversight in all aspects of ministry, including service, personal ministry and Godly character.

Bill offers a wide range of writings and teachings from deliverance, to experiencing presence of God and developing Apostolic cutting edge Church structure. Drawing on the power of the Holy Spirit through years of experience in Revival, Spiritual Sensitivity, and deliverance ministry, Bill now focuses mainly on pursuing the Presence of God and breaking the power of the devil off of people's lives.

His books 48 and counting has since helped many people to overcome the spirits and curses of Satan. For more information or to keep up with Bill's latest releases, please visit www.revivalwavesofgloryministries.com. To contact Bill, feel free to follow him on twitter @revivalwaves.

Recommended Books

By Bill Vincent
Overcoming Obstacles
Glory: Pursuing God's Presence
Defeating the Demonic Realm
Increasing Your Prophetic Gift
Increase Your Anointing
Keys to Receiving Your Miracle
The Supernatural Realm
Waves of Revival
Increase of Revelation and Restoration
The Resurrection Power of God
Discerning Your Call of God
Apostolic Breakthrough
Glory: Increasing God's Presence
Love is Waiting – Don't Let Love Pass You By
The Healing Power of God
Glory: Expanding God's Presence
Receiving Personal Prophecy
Signs and Wonders
Signs and Wonders Revelations
Children Stories
The Rapture
The Secret Place of God's Power
Building a Prototype Church
Breakthrough of Spiritual Strongholds
Glory: Revival Presence of God
Overcoming the Power of Lust
Glory: Kingdom Presence of God

Transitioning to the Prototype Church
The Stronghold of Jezebel
Healing After Divorce
A Closer Relationship With God
Cover Up and Save Yourself
Desperate for God's Presence
The War for Spiritual Battles
Spiritual Leadership
Global Warning
Millions of Churches
Destroying the Jezebel Spirit
Awakening of Miracles
Deception and Consequences Revealed
Are You a Follower of Christ
Don't Let the Enemy Steal from You!
A Godly Shaking
The Unsearchable Riches of Christ
Heaven's Court System
Satan's Open Doors
Armed for Battle
The Wrestler
Spiritual Warfare: Complete Collection
Growing In the Prophetic
Faith
The Angry Fighter's Story
Understanding Heaven's Court System

Web Site:
www.revivalwavesofgloryministries.com

I Would Love to Hear from You

As a writer, I welcome your input.

One way to really bless me, however, is to write an honest review of any length of this book on Amazon. This helps others decide if they should buy this book. Writing a review costs you nothing, and it is one way to let me know that you enjoyed the book. Please take the time to do so, even if you have never written one before.

www.ingramcontent.com/pod-product-compliance
Lightning Source LLC
Chambersburg PA
CBHW052117070526
44584CB00017B/2529